Present! Connect!

Present! Connect!

Create and Deliver Presentations That Capture, Entertain, and Connect to ANY Audience

Tom Guggino

 BUSINESS EXPERT PRESS

Present! Connect!: Create and Deliver Presentations That Capture, Entertain, and Connect to ANY Audience

Cover image licensed by Ingram Image, StockPhotoSecrets.com

First published in 2020 by
Business Expert Press, LLC
222 East 46th Street, New York, NY 10017
www.businessexpertpress.com

ISBN-13: 978-1-95152-724-2 (paperback)
ISBN-13: 978-1-95152-725-9 (e-book)

Business Expert Press Business Career Development

Collection ISSN: 2642-2123 (print)
Collection ISSN: 2642-2131 (electronic)

Cover and interior design by Exeter Premedia Services Private Ltd., Chennai, India

First edition: 2020

10 9 8 7 6 5 4 3 2 1

Printed in the United States of America.

Dedicated to Deanie Guggino
Who was with me from the start, was my inspiration and taught me how to love life

Abstract

Most people are born with the skills needed to become a successful presenter, but they don't use them. When they do learn how to use these skills, they begin to enjoy the challenge and then the successful outcome of a focused, thoughtful, and informative presentation. This is the premise of author Tom Guggino's career as a leading presentation coach.

As a former stand-up comedian, Tom applies the secrets of communicating your passion, commitment, and unique personal style. He has developed The Presentation Process to make professionals, executives, and students become effective presenters who enjoy making a presentation that fulfills its promise.

Tom Guggino is a presentation coach who shares with readers his acclaimed knowledge as a premier practitioner of helping people bring out their talents to become a successful presenter. He adapts the basic premises and applications of winning over an audience, from initial contact to the exciting finish.

Tom shows how a speaker will know when the audience is engaged by creating a positive sensory environment. The presenter will know the profile of the audience, why they are there, and what they want to take away with them from the presenter's message.

PRESENT! CONNECT! Combines a one-on-one conversational style with lively graphics and case studies that can improve your presentation skills quickly. Get ready to tap into your successful skills and start having fun presenting.

Keywords

Secrets; successful skills; effective presenter; stand-up comedian; winning over an audience; unique personal style; conversational style

Contents

Preface

The idea for this book came from my desire to share the techniques and skills I learned and developed over 25 years of coaching clients how to customize presentations for audiences to not only receive a message but to perceive a message. When a message is perceived, the audience internalizes it and takes it with them. They understand the intent and the application of the message. They know the value and how it fits into what they already know.

I have coached clients from a variety of fields and markets ranging from architects to doctors to corporate executives to teachers to doctoral candidates. Since I began my career as a comic in a comedy team called "McAndrews and Gino," I wanted to bring the secrets and tricks that professional performers use to entertain, manage, and delight their audiences. Some of these techniques are not known outside of the professional world but are quickly learned and can have a significant impact on audiences. Knowing these techniques and secrets can help any presenter have more confidence, prepare presentation quicker and have more control over an audience's reactions.

As I watched presenters struggle through the process of developing a presentation, I wanted to find a way to make it easier for them. I wanted to make the process quicker and shorter. The *Presentation Process* is a unique process that focuses on an individual's personality and style. It uses a self-critique and self-evaluation method to create immediate awareness, feedback, and insights into one's content and style when making a presentation. The *Presentation Process* can be used for any presentation regardless of the purpose or audience.

It has helped many people in a variety of fields such as hospitality, sales, design and construction, health care, telecommunications, and education.

I have organized the book into chapters that can be used independently or in sequence. The goal is to give practical tips and techniques that can be used immediately and produce results quickly.

To match my coaching style of customizing techniques and advice for each person personally, I have arranged the content of the book into the process of how presenters should prepare for a presentation. I believe presenting is an art and, like any art, should be practiced to develop a body habit that can be used each time there is a presentation. Body habits enable people to do something without thinking about it. Freeing yourself from thinking about the process of presenting can focus you on performing and allow you to connect to the audience.

I believe that everyone has a power inside of them that they can use when presenting—a power that is intense and can demand the audience to look and connect with you. In performing, we call it "Flashing on the audience," which means to bring a burst of energy when performing. It's a feeling we get in the audience from an actor, singer, or comedian that pulls us to them. It's that feeling you get when you see your favorite performer, and suddenly, time doesn't exist. That's the power everyone has, and now you can learn how to use it.

I've authored this book in the same way that I coach my clients. I wanted my writing style to reflect the conversation style I use in coaching. It's informal and pragmatic and gets to techniques and skills that can be applied quickly. Like you, my clients are busy and want tips that are easily understood and easily applied to their next presentation.

So, get ready to forget about yourself and *become one with the audience*. Get ready to learn how to enjoy presenting!

CHAPTER 1

The Presentation Process

It's 9:00 am, and George is ready to make his presentation to a potential client. He enters the room and shakes hands with everyone. They appear friendly but are holding back their feelings so as not to tip their hand as to who they might pick for the project. George begins. Before coming here, George had practiced—at least he thought he did. On the train, he gathered his thoughts—tried to think about how he would do it when he was in front of the client. He looked good in his mind.

As George proceeded with his presentation, he suddenly got the feeling that it wasn't going well. He was telling them how excited he was and how gratified he felt to make the list of companies they wanted to see. But now he felt as if their interest was waning. He thought to himself, "What am I doing wrong? I know this material, and I know I'm the best choice for the project, and yet I haven't grabbed their attention. They're not listening to me. I didn't make a connection with them."

George wrapped up his talk, and politely left the room. Carrying his materials down the hall, he felt as if he had just missed it, and yet it was another presentation with all too familiar results. George consoled himself with the thought that the client must have selected someone else, and the interview process was just for show—a sham. He asked himself, "Why were they looking for someone to do the project when it was already decided? It must have been an inside job." George went back to his office and started to prepare for a new presentation, hoping that the next one would be better. Maybe the next time the client will listen and understand why George and his firm should get the project.

Poor George, he works so hard, and yet he just can't see why he doesn't get selected for the project. Why aren't successful presentations based on hard work? Then George would win every time. But they're not.

George is like so many people who just can't figure out why their presentations fail. He can't figure out how the client decides on who they

McANDREWS AND GINO

Figure 1.1 McAndrews and Gino promotional picture
Photo: Guggino/Personal Archives

wanted to work with or how he can connect with them to show that he understands their needs.

Most presenters blame the audience when a presentation fails instead of looking at what they did. The rejection they feel makes them angry, and therefore, they search for blame.

Being in show business for nine years in a comedy team called McAndrews and Gino, I know what it feels like to be in front of an audience. I have failed more than most presenters have tried, but I have also succeeded more than most presenters have tried. I became a technician at knowing audiences and how they react. I discovered how to influence and lead an audience to where I wanted to take them. Now I am going to share those secrets with you.

Figure 1.2 Pug the dog loves to get petted!
Photo: Guggino/Personal Archives

Most audiences want you to succeed. They want you to tell them something they don't know or make them laugh or take them some place they have never been before.

Relaxing the audience

As a young comic, I realized that the audience was nervous or anxious when we were being introduced. They didn't know us, and probably never heard of us. The audience was worried that we were not going to be funny. So, to relax the audience, we created an opening sketch that had me playing a dog in which my wife, Deanie, had sent to guard dog school and now wants to give me, Pug the dog, a test to see what I had learned.

As soon as she called me on stage, the audience started to laugh because I was wearing a toy army helmet and was excited to see her. She began to pet me on the back, and I immediately turned over, and she stroked my stomach, which quickly brought out my tongue with sounds of extreme pleasure. Of course, I failed the test miserably and howled in disappointment. The sketch never failed because it was so animated and over the top that the audience immediately relaxed and laughed. Now, remember this sketch was for the audience and not for us.

We knew we were funny, but the audience didn't know that, and so they had anxiety about new comics. If you ever witnessed a comic failing, then you know how bad that can feel. You just want to disappear because you feel so bad for the performer. So, by thinking about the audience and not about ourselves, we were able to relax the audience and show them that we were funny and that they would enjoy the show even though they had never heard of us.

Our friend George concentrated on himself and not on his audience and missed the opportunity to show his audience that he knew more about them than they realized. **Speaking to an audience's self-interest is the first way to establish a connection with them.** Presenters who know how to discover the insights into their audience never fail because the one thing that drives all of us is our self-interest. It's not hard once you know the secrets contained in my *Presentation Process*, which will lead you step-by-step. But before we get to the *Presentation Process*, let's look at presentations in general and how people receive messages.

Many of us must do presentations. Maybe you were told to do one by your supervisor, or you have an idea that you want others to hear. You might want to enhance your image in the company. Or maybe it's your job to communicate messages to others. No matter what the reason, presentations are the way we communicate to groups of people and individuals. So, unless you're a mime, as in pantomime with a white face and a derby hat, you're going to have to speak.

Speaking in front of an audience is what scares people. So many people believe it is a test of fire, where everyone is looking at you, listening to how you say every word, and judging you while you talk. Well, I hate to tell you, that's not what's happening. Most people in your audience are not thinking about you. They are thinking about themselves. In fact, that's what most of us do every minute of every day; we think about our needs, wants, and desires. We, humans, are "self-interested, heat-seeking missiles."

So instead of judging someone, we simply start our self-talk in our minds and ignore whatever or whoever doesn't interest us. The real problem is not people judging us but how to connect with an audience, so they listen to us and don't start their self-talk.

> The real problem is not people judging us but how to connect with an audience, so they listen to us and don't start their self-talk.

Knowing just a few simple principles can make your presentations connect and stand out. They can make your presentation sound like you, and let people understand who you are and why it's so important to listen to you. Sounds easy? It is. I have been coaching people for over 25 years, and all my clients have something in common. They are different. They have unique personalities and perceptions about their work and the world. It's this uniqueness that makes a presentation succeed.

The more we allow an audience to know us, the more they are drawn into our story and message. For this reason, I have developed the *Presentation Process, a process with just four steps that can heighten interest and make content come alive and applications easily understood.*

The Presentation Process

1. *Developing a client or audience strategy*
2. *Creating an opening/summarizing the theme*
3. *Selecting the content to support your opening*
4. *Performance using both the voice and the body*

These are the elements that will help you understand and create messages and presentations that will connect to your audience.

Using the *Presentation Process*, you will be able to develop a self-critique and self-evaluation method, which creates immediate awareness and feedback. It will enhance your confidence and help you "tell a story" in a more personalized and relaxed manner. You'll know the secrets of how to change your behavior, especially behavior performed in front of an audience.

What makes the *Presentation Process* so successful is that it emphasizes working within your personality and style. Most people are successful in their professions and the *Presentation Process* can show you how to apply your own proven skills to improve your presentations. By concentrating on your successful abilities that you already use in other situations, you will be more trusting in examining your presentations and recognize the changes you must make.

> I have coached hundreds of people in a variety of fields. The *Presentation Process* is a proven process that will dramatically improve your presentation skills and help you to create successful presentations that connect to an audience the first time and every time.

With my *Presentation Process*, you will find that improvements are quick and easy to achieve once you understand the four easy steps. The *Presentation Process* will improve your presentation skills, reduce your preparation time, and make you more relaxed. Bringing a conversational style to your presentations, and making the content more organized and more comfortable to deliver, and helping you to use visuals to heighten interest and create drama.

Changing or modifying behavior is never easy, especially behavior that is performed in front of an audience. What makes my *Presentation Process* successful is its emphasis on identifying your personality and style. It will show you how to apply your proven personal skills to deliver a polished presentation that grabs the audience at the beginning and holds their attention for its duration.

The first time I meet with a client in a presentation session, I say, "I am not going to change your personality or make you a comic or make you be someone else. I am going to work within your personality because that's where your comfort zone is." Something that I have discovered in my coaching is that your presentation style should be as close to your personality as possible. Many presenters think they must be someone else when they present. Some believe they should imitate a style that they saw or heard someone else do.

When it comes to presenting, the best style is one based on your talents and perceptions. You already have strong skills that you use every day. Those skills should be the foundation of how you present. When you are yourself, and in your comfort zone, beautiful things can happen. You act naturally and project confidence and credibility to the audience.

Being relaxed is especially crucial in showing the audience who you are and the passion you have for your subject.

The *Presentation Process* has helped such professionals as architects, engineers, doctors, health care system coordinators, corporate executives and managers, community relations personnel, politicians, sales representatives, and educators. Throughout the 25 years of applying my *Presentation Process* to people like you, consistent and positive results have become evident:

- Everyone's presentation skills improved.
- The presentation prep time was less.
- The content of the presentations was better organized and delivered.
- Presenters were more relaxed and conversational in their style.
- Presenters better integrated their talk tracks with their visuals to emphasize the subject matter.

I will show you how to discover your comfort zone and how easy it is to use in all your presentations. *The real task is to find out what you can personally bring to a presentation that will connect and excite an audience.*

CHAPTER 2

Preparing to Deliver a Presentation

When I coach a client, I always ask, "How do you prepare a presentation? Do you just start writing? Do you sit and think before you write? Do you begin at the beginning, the end, or in the middle?" Most presenters want to dive into the preparation right away. They want to start writing everything they know about a particular subject, so the audience will know they know the subject matter. That's like going to a movie, and instead of the opening scene, there is an interview with the screen writer. He tells the audience everything he knows about the subject of the movie and why he was qualified to write the script. How long would you last before you would leave? Not long, I'm sure. If you're writing everything you know when you're preparing a presentation, then you're working way too hard.

Other presenters will put off the prep until it's close to the presentation time and then panic and start writing anything feverishly. They will fill up pages with material that is not connected or has little to do with the interest of the audience.

Still others will sit frozen, unable to think because the task seems overwhelming. They will start, then stop, then start, and then stop again. They think to themselves, "What am I going to do? I'm going to make a fool of myself. Everyone will find me out. I'm a fake. I'm not qualified to do this."

It might surprise some people, but many professional performers have the same anxiety before doing a show. They think they are not talented and will be found out to be a fake. When I performed at the Comedy Store in Los Angeles, many of the comics were panicking before going on. The bathroom was a very crowded place, filled with comics doing all kinds of bodily functions. And these are people who performed almost every night. Even the best actors on Broadway have anxiety when first

Figure 2.1 Preparation is essential to a successful presentation!
Photo: Deagreez/Getty Images

cast. They think I couldn't possibly do the part. They find it hard to memorize lines.

A client who doesn't prepare

I had a client, who was the CEO of a large organization, tell me that he doesn't prepare anything. He just goes out there and sees what happens. He liked to wing it. Well, he winged it one too many times and started getting negative feedback from his board. That's when I got the panic call asking me to help him. My advice is unless you are an incredibly talented presenter with years of experience, winging it is dangerous if you want to succeed in communicating a successful message.

The purpose of preparation is to help the audience understand your message. It is time you take to create a guide for the audience to become immersed in your theme. Immersing an audience is like dunking them in the water where they can feel the emotional impact of your presentation. A time where you can create an experience that the audience will take with them and tell others. A time to develop stories, visuals examples, and yes laughs that will make your audience want to listen to everything you say. Sound exciting? Well, the *Presentation Process* will take you through a process that is easy and shows you how the pros do it.

Common Interest

Audiences have many things in common. They want to be entertained, engaged, and drawn into whatever they are watching, listening, or participating in. Think about the movies, TV shows, books, and even commercials that grab your attention. Usually, they attract you with something you like and know. You engage because it touches your self-interest. It's the same with a presentation.

As a presenter, you must find the self-interest of the audience for them to listen. The one question you should always ask yourself while you are preparing a presentation is, *Why should they listen?* It is an important question that will guide you to select content and help you in arranging material.

Preparing for a presentation can be scary and hard, and for some people, something to be avoided at all costs. The value of preparation is that it allows you to explore and experiment with ideas and concepts that will excite your audience. There's nothing better than seeing your message accepted by an audience. The feeling is something that once you've experienced it, you will want to experience again and again. When I performed and felt the audience with me, following my every gesture, it was intoxicating and powerful.

Knowing you have the audience

We did a silent film pantomime called *The Pirate*, where I save the pretty young damsel from the devilish Blue Beard, the Pirate. In the end, after I had lost a sword fight to Blue Beard Pirate, I raise my hands and offer the pretty young damsel to him. The damsel hesitantly goes up to Blue Beard and gently kisses him. Blue Beard rejects her. With my hands still in the air, I slowly point to myself. He accepts; I pantomime kissing him, and he like me. So, I merrily go off stage with him. The audience loved it because they were totally into the scene and loved the turn against me. They were watching me so closely that a small gesture like pointing to myself with my forefinger on my right hand was a big laugh.

Preparation allows you to research the audience's self-interest so, when you present, they feel you are talking directly to them. The audience feels like you know them. When an audience connects to a presenter in this way, magical things can happen.

How the Brain works

When it comes to audiences' reactions, there are a few things you should know about how our brains work. First, we don't see what we think we see, and we don't hear what we think we hear.

There is a book written by two neuroscientists who interview magicians about their magic acts. The book is called *Sleighs of Mind* by Stephen L. Macknik and Susana Martinez-Conde, with Sandra Blakeslee, what the neuroscience of magic reveals about our everyday deceptions. In the book, the magicians explain their tricks, revealing everything, and then the neuroscientists explain how our brains reacted to the trick. It explains that the audience is part of the trick and that their response is essential for the trick to work. Likewise, presenters understanding how an audience receives messages can be just as critical to the success of a presentation.

When a presenter begins a presentation, audiences give the presenter about 20-45 seconds before they start their internal self-talk. They don't consciously make a judgment not to listen, but they react to not hearing anything of interest. So, they begin to think about themselves and the business or personnel things going on in their lives.

Most presenters believe that an audience will judge them, but that is not true. Audiences focused on themselves will ignore a presenter rather than judge them. That's how our brain works. *So, prepare a presentation that includes the audience's self-interest, and you will always have their attention.*

CHAPTER 3

How to Ensure Your Presentation Won't Fail Technically

When it comes to presenting, the old saying still applies: "What can go wrong will go wrong."

The worst nightmare every presenter has is that when they are presenting, the speaker support that they are relying on doesn't work. You know the scenario: you're just beginning the presentation, and the microphone doesn't work, or the projector suddenly stops showing your slides or shows your slides order.

What do you do? Start tap dancing or go to the hand puppets? No, the answer lies in your preparation for the presentation. How do you ensure that what must work does work? Well, the first thing is you must be in control of all the hardware and software that you are going to use. You must be what I call "self-contained." That means that no matter what happens, you have a backup for what might happen.

Most professional performers want to be in control of how they are presenting to the audience. That's the way they protect their images and brand so carefully. Did you ever notice the trucks parked outside when you went to a concert or show? Those trucks contain everything the performers need to do the show. They leave little to chance because they can't fail. The same goes for any presentation. If it can't fail, then you must prepare it so it doesn't fail.

Here are a few simple things to do when you are preparing your presentation, so it doesn't fail.

> Professional performers leave very little to chance because they can't fail.

1. Make a copy of your presentation on a USB memory drive.

To be sure that you can always recover your presentation, making a copy is a prudent thing to do. Many times, there can be conflicts with the connections or with the software if you are not using your computer or device. You can also make a mistake with the presentation even with your device and need to reload the presentation.

2. Do you know where you will be presenting, and do you have a description of the location or space?

It seems obvious, but you would be surprised to know how many presenters don't know. It's always a good idea to see the location before doing a presentation in the space. You want to check the room for electrical outlets to see where they are and how far they will be from your computer and equipment. Also, check to see if they are two-prong or three-prong plug outlets. If they are two-prong, then you might need a three-prong adapter that lets you plug a three-prong cord into a two-prong outlet.

You also want to check out the arrangement of the room and where the audience will be concerning to where you will be presenting. You want the audience to be in front of you with clear sight lines to you and the screen.

3. Make sure you do a technical run-through in the room before you present.

Another fail-safe idea is to test out all the equipment and software in the room before you present. For your tech run-through, plug everything in and do a few minutes of your presentation. This way, you can test the sound, microphone, projector, handheld slide advance/pointer, and your slides. You want to be sure that the sound levels are suitable for the room and that your slides are clear and in order. If you are using a handheld mic, you want to be sure you hold it close to your mouth, but do not touch your lips. If you have cards or notes, practice holding the mic and changing the cards or notes as you present.

4. What to pack and carry with you for a presentation.

Most producers in the performing arts know that there are always unexpected problems when performing. They do everything they can to make sure they have prepared the performance, so it doesn't fail. They prepare for the unexpected things that might happen. They want to have equipment and people ready so they have options when something goes wrong. As a presenter, you also should be prepared for the unexpected and carry equipment and materials with you, so you have options when something happens.

- Your laptop computer or another device
- An AC power strip
- Electrical extension cords with three to two adapters
- A small flashlight
- Your slide changer/pointer
- Your projector
- Handouts of your slides
- Small speakers
- Batteries—double AA and triple AAA

5. Checking that everything works.

When you are preparing your presentation, you should do a run-through with all the equipment connected. As mentioned, do it in the space where you will be delivering your presentation. This set up will tell you if any connections might interfere with your equipment. If that isn't possible, then do a run-through off-site.

A complete run-through means

- Turning on the projector
- Testing the speakers
- Turning on the computer to be used
- Looking at all slides and videos

Testing all software and hardware materials will give you control over the elements that support your presentation. It will also eliminate one more thing from the check list.

One final note: you must take full responsibility for a presentation to be fail-safe.

As music fans, we have all seen our favorite bands in arenas and clubs and never thought about what the preparations were behind the scenes to make sure the concert never failed. The people behind the scenes are called roadies. They are the people who make everything work. You must become your own roadie and make sure that everything works, so your presentation never fails.

Making your presentation fail-safe will have another benefit. It will help you focus on your presentation. Not being distracted by thinking, "Did I check that?" or "Do I have that?" will free you to concentrate on your presentation. It will also help in relaxing you, knowing that everything is working and ready. **Being relaxed is the way to become present with the audience.**

CHAPTER 4

Why Do Presentations Fail?

Some things are obvious; others are not.

- Lack of skills
- Content not clear
- Can't hear the presenter
- Body language distracts
- Recording your presentation

Lack of Skills

In our opening story, George was disappointed at the reaction he got from his audience. He was talking about what he thought the client ought to know and not about what the client wanted to hear, their self-interest in the project. He blamed the audience and thought it wasn't his fault. So many times, presenters, like George, don't understand why their presentations fail.

There are many reasons why a presentation fails. The most common is when a presenter fails to make a connection to the audience. Some of the causes for this might be obvious, but others are not so evident.

The most common reason is when presenters are self-consumed and are not focusing on the audience. They become anxious about how they will perform and worried that the audience would reject them. They get stuck in their internal self-talk, which can become so intense, they freeze and can't present. Once they begin their presentation, they communicate their anxiety to the audience, and the audience stops listening.

Stopping negative internal self-talk is not easy. It takes practice and knowing how to become external. Turning off your self-talk is crucial if you are going to be present with the audience. **Being present is the first step in connecting to an audience.**

Figure 4.1 "Have you heard?" always works!
Photo: Bim/Getty Images

Content Not Clear

The second reason why presentations fail is not making the content clear to the audience. Presenters assume that the audience can apply the subject matter, so they don't create examples, metaphors, or stories to illustrate their content. Most of the information we receive daily comes to us as examples, metaphors, and stories. The most famous phrase to get someone to listen is to ask, "Have you heard?" The person immediately begins to listen and replies, "No. I haven't. What is it?" Audiences want to know how the content of a presentation relates to them. How it affects them, helps them, or makes their lives easier. *Content must connect with the self-interest of the audience.* Presenters who include the self-interest of the audience in their presentations will connect to their audience.

> The most famous phrase to get someone to listen
> is to ask "Have you heard?"

Can't Hear the Presenter

Another simple but common mistake is that the audience can't hear the presenter. The presenter's voice is too low, or they talk too fast, or constantly look down at their notes, or at the screen to check their slides. The voice is an essential element in a successful presentation.

A voice that commands attention and fills the space can help a presenter connect immediately with an audience. Anyone can have a good presentation voice if you learn how to use your diaphragm when you present. A presentation voice is different than a conversation voice. *A conversation voice lies in your throat, but a presentation voice is supported with air from the diaphragm, giving the voice a fuller sound. This same technique is used by singers.*

Body Language Distracts

Body language is another reason why presentations fail. The audience becomes distracted by some repetitive movement the presenter is making. The distraction overwhelms the message the presenter is trying to convey. It draws the audience's attention away from listening to the presenter and on some physical action that the presenter is doing.

It could be that the presenter is holding on to the podium too tightly or sways back and forth while talking. It could be a physical tick that the presenter is unaware of and can't understand why the audience is distracted.

A salesman not selling

There was a salesman once, who had the habit of shaking his head "no" when he asked the client if they wanted to buy his product. He couldn't understand why he wasn't making sales. It's tough to answer "yes" when someone is shaking their head "no." Try it sometime. Ask a friend a question that requires a "yes" answer, but when you ask the question, shake your head no before you ask it and see what response you get from your friend.

Recording Your Presentation

There is a connection between what we say and how we say it. We either convey a single message or send competing messages to the receiver. Multiple messages confuse the receiver and subvert the message we are trying to communicate. Being aware of what our bodies are doing is necessary if we are going to self-manage our body language. *Recording a presentation is the first step in becoming aware of our body language.*

I routinely record my clients in private sessions. Most of them are surprised the first time they see themselves on camera. They're not used to seeing how they look on camera, but they come to understand that to be a successful presenter, they must know how others perceive them.

As a presenter, knowing how others see you, can help you in managing what you do and how you do it. The purpose of recording yourself is to compare your internal perception with what you see on the recording. Knowing how others see you can relax you because it will put you in control of what you project. *Controlling all the messages we send is vital if our messages and presentations are to succeed.*

CHAPTER 5

Elements of a Successful Presentation

Knowing How to Make an Audience Respond

When a speaker succeeds, it seems so obvious. The audience and the presenter connect and are one in rhythm, message, and understanding. There is a sense of agreement between the audience and the presenter that they are one and can move in any direction as a single mind. When it happens, it is magical. If you have ever experienced it, you know the feeling of the emotional high that generates between the presenter and the audience.

Yet as magical as it may seem, it doesn't happen by chance. Behind every successful presentation, there is a conscience design that uses a process that enables the presenter to know the audience and reduces the risk of failure. Successful presenters do not take risks. They control all the elements of their message and their performance.

An excellent example of a successful presentation is a scene in the Broadway play and movie *The Music Man* by Meredith Willson. The scene is "Ya Got Trouble," and the lead character, Harold Hill, informs the people that they have *Trouble—a Pool Hall and that starts with P, and that rhymes with T and that stands for Trouble.* The presentation is compelling because he knows his audience so well. He knows that the people in this small town won't spend money on themselves but will spend money to keep their kids safe after school. His presentation reveals all the dangers that are lurking in the pool hall and how it will affect their kids. His style is like a preacher warning them of impending evil that's coming to get their children. He knows that they will recognize the style since they see it every Sunday in their churches.

Using what he knows about his audience, he brings them to a feverish pitch and ready to do anything to save their children. His solution will be

"In the future, that should produce thousands of PhD theses."

Figure 5.1 *It's important to know your audience!*
Cartoon: Becall, Aaron/Cartoon Stock

uniforms for a boy's band that he is pretending to sell. It is available on YouTube, and when you see it, compare how he uses all the elements of a successful presentation.

Elements of a Successful Presentation

1. *The subject matter and content design include the self-interest of the audience.*

   - Every successful presentation is customizes for its audience. That's how presenters engage the audience.

2. *The subject matter is clear and concise and shows connections between ideas.*

   - Making connections between ideas allows the audience to digest the topic and gives them time to make connections to what they already know.

CHAPTER 6

Openings

Connecting as Soon as You Start to Talk

- Openings are summaries of your entire presentation.
- Giving the reasons why an audience should listen.
- Creating interest and connections at the beginning.
- Speak directly to the audience's self-interest.

Openings Are Summaries of Your Entire Presentation

When presenters start to talk, the audience gives them about 20-45 seconds before they stop listening and start their internal self-talk. So how do successful presenters immediately connect with an audience and keep their attention?

They begin with something that the audience finds interesting. It is something that speaks to the self-interest of the audience. I call it an opening, and it is a critical part of a presentation. It is the first thing the presenter says after being introduced. It is not introductory remarks like "Thank you for inviting me, and it is such a pleasure being here." That says to the audience you haven't started, so they don't have to listen.

Audiences intrinsically know the cues. They understand when presenters are connecting with them, and they know when they are not. Audiences come with expectations about a presentation. In a way, they are trying to outguess the presenter and the way their presentation might go.

Playing with expectations in a classroom
I was coaching high school teachers on their presentations in the classroom, and I asked them, "How do you start your classes each day?" They said, "I take attendance, collect homework, and then

start class." It took about 5 to 10 minutes. I said, "So the students know the class hasn't started so they don't have to pay attention." The teacher said, "Yes." I said I wanted to try something that might get the students' attention going even before they started the class. The teacher was an American history teacher covering the Civil War. The teacher agreed. I said, "Why don't you use that time before you start the class to get their attention. While you are taking the attendance and collecting homework, show pictures from the Civil War in random order on the screen in the classroom and see how long it takes before one of your students asks you about the images on the screen."

He reported back that it took about two to three minutes before someone asked, "What are those pictures for? And do we have to know them?" The teacher then said, "What pictures?" The student said, "Those on the screen." The teacher said, "Which one?" Suddenly a conversation started involving more students.

What happened? Well, our brains demand order and can't tolerate disorder for too long. Even when there is no apparent order to what we see, our minds will create order. The students had to know why the pictures were on the screen, and if it meant anything, they should know.

Being aware of how our brains react to stimuli can be very helpful in creating an opening. Audiences come with expectations about what they are about to see and hear. *Knowing the expectations of the audience is an important element when creating an opening.* Audiences create expectations from the title of a presentation or having knowledge of the topic or knowing something about the speaker. As a presenter, you should know as much as you can about your audience's expectations.

- *Examine the expectations of the audience.*

If you want to know how to find out about the expectations of your audience, start with contacting the person who is arranging the presentation. Ask a few questions about what they believe is the expectation of the audience. Another source to consider is, do you know anyone who might be part of the audience. Or, do you know someone who knows the members of the audience?

Asking these sources about what they believe the audience expects can give you insights and information you can use in creating a customized opening for your audience. Good openings can: surprise, excite, and engage the audience to listen. Openings should generate the reason for why your audience should listen. Successful presenters always give their audience a reason to listen and continue to remind the audience throughout the entire presentation.

- *Is your audience motivated or unmotivated?*

A motivated audience is one who **must** get the information that's being presented. They need it and will listen no matter how the topic is displayed. An example is a presentation on "How do you get paid?" The audience will tolerate almost anything to get the information. They are motivated because the subject matter is important to them.

Unfortunately, a motivated audience is not a the typical audience for presentations. Most audiences are unmotivated. They might know something about the subject matter or nothing at all. With unmotivated audiences, presenters must start with something that engages the audience quickly, something that speaks directly to the self-interest of the audience.

- *The audience's level of understanding about the topic.*

Knowing the audience's level of understanding can help in customizing the content of your presentation.

- *The three levels of an Audience's knowledge are*

1. *Expert*
2. *Novice*
3. *Hearing the topic for the first time*

Presenters should consider these levels when deciding which content to include in their presentations.

An *expert audience* knows the topic well, and therefore it must be an in-depth approach to the content and contain even new content to keep their interest. Some content, like definitions, references, and leaders in the field, can be assumed to be known.

A *novice audience* only has a light understanding of the topic. Therefor use definitions, visuals, and metaphors as examples to help them follow the topic.

If your *audience is hearing the topic for the first time*, then to engage them, you must use examples and references that are familiar and easily recognizable. Look for examples from the audience's personal or business lives or popular culture.

One time, a student wanted to come up with an analogy that would help describe their job as head of dining at a large university. They decided to compare the process of preparing meals for students to the battle of Gettysburg. They described how everyone they managed had to know their function and how the units had to be ready to respond to deliver the food hot to the students.

By using a popular historical event, the student was able to draw the audience in and show the organizational skills necessary to succeed.

- *What do you want your audience to feel or do?*

Knowing what you want your audience to do or feel after a presentation is the final question you should ask in researching your opening. Most performers and presenters begin at the end work backward. They decide what should be the call to action or what is the emotional feeling they want their audience to experience. If it is a call to action, then what are the motivational elements necessary to bring the audience to want to do something?

What are the stories you can use to move an audience to action? It is easier to work backward when you know the ending because it creates a road map to get there. Just like planning a road trip, it is easier to understand what your destination is before you start so that the best route can be selected.

Creating an emotional response from an audience is similar. Knowing where you want to leave an audience emotionally can be carefully planned after deciding what the final emotional feeling ought to be. Is it a feeling of "I didn't know that" or "That was a real surprise" or "I never realized how challenging that is" or "That was fun"? Decide the emotional feeling you want to achieve, then design a path to that response using examples and stories to experience that feeling.

3. *The style is close to the personality of the presenter.*
- Unless you're an actor, don't become someone you're not.
- Projecting who you are is a critical element of a successful presentation.
- Being relaxed and in your comfort zone shows confidence and credibility.

4. *Delivery elements.*
- The voice is relaxed and understandable.
- The audience can easily hear the presenter.
- Body language is natural, and nothing distracts.
- The gestures support the delivery.
- The appearance of the presenter supports the message.
- The presenter has dressed appropriately, and the language supports the presenter's message.

5. *The presentation messages.*
- Messages organized in a logical order for the sender—receiver to work.
- The messages are applied using comparisons that the audience knows.
- The examples used help the audience visualize the information.

Deanie and I performed at a club in Denver. When it came time to do improvisations, we ask for a suggestion that could happen on a wedding night. A man in the audience said, "Getting lost in the boondocks!" His wife shouted, "Yea; he wouldn't stop and ask for directions." The audience started laughing, so I knew this was a good suggestion. The next thing I did was to see how long I could talk to the couple before I had to start the improvisation. Everything the couple told me was going to be the lines we were going to use in our improvised sketch. I knew what the ending was going to be, 'Oh my. I think we're lost in the boondocks!'

We did the improvised sketch, and the audience laughed and thought we were so talented. The audience didn't realize that they had told us what they thought was funny. We listened, and that's what we did.

Knowing your audience is the path to a successful performance.

Understanding the elements of successful presentations will help you create compelling presentations that communicate your message to the audience. Audiences want you to lead them. They want to know how your message will help them and how it will change their lives. Once an audience recognizes that your message is for them, they will connect with you.

Although the purposes and audiences may defer, all successful presentations contain these elements and create a special bond with the audience.

The *Presentation Process* will help you create a successful presentation. The first two steps in the process are knowing your audience and creating an opening.

Awnings are more than just awnings

A client had to prepare a presentation for the association of awning manufacturers. He was searching for an opening. We talked about the audience and examined who they were and what their expectations were about the presentation. The audience was made up of different age groups from millennials to senior salespeople.

1. We discussed what the audience should feel after the presentation.
2. My client wanted the audience to experience pride in working with awnings.
3. Whether they manufactured or sold them to customers.
4. We started to examine what shelters like awnings do and what was the value to the customer.
5. The obvious was they provided shade to a deck or patio.
6. Awnings allowed people to experience events outside.
7. They invite their families and friends to a variety of social and family gatherings.

Suddenly my client said, "Memories"! I said, "Yes, an awning enables people to experience good times with the people they love. It enables people to create memories for a lifetime." We had it. We elevated the idea of an awning from just being taken for granted to feeling pride in working with awnings. He then wrote the opening and started to take his audience on a journey of discovery about what they did and how it affects their customers. They were no longer only awning manufacturers and salespeople, but people who enable their customers to create memories for a lifetime.

His opening was successful, and the audience was with him from the start of his presentation. He lifted them from ordinary awning salespeople and manufacturers to people whose job created opportunities for their customers. *His opening related to anyone who feels creating memories is important in their lives.*

CHAPTER 7

Content and Body Language

What You Say and How You Say It

- Dealing with content to support your opening
- The logic of messages
- Writing to be spoken and not to be read
- How to control body language

Dealing with Content to Support Your Opening

The Logic of a Message

One of the things I want to do is to help people save time in preparing for presentations.

When people prepare content for a presentation, they usually begin with all the content available on a topic. Dealing with all the content available can take time, lots of time. After searching for all the material about a topic, you still won't have a guide for using the material in your presentation.

Instead of starting with arranging the content on the topic without a purpose, the first step ought to be to create an *opening* based on the research you've done in getting to know your audience. Then the content you select is only that content that supports your opening.

The opening sets up the criteria for the content you will prepare. Knowing what you need to support your opening will cut down on your preparation time and help you to focus on developing ways to express your content through stories and examples. Narrowing the content can help the audience understand your topic better because they won't have to slug through the information to get to the main points of your presentation. Selecting content that only supports your opening will help you understand what content is essential in presenting your topic.

As a presenter, you must guide your audience through the information and create dramatic connections that will lead your audience to want more. Answering the question, "Why should the audience want to listen?" is found in the opening and supported through the content selected to demonstrate your topic.

1. Creating a logic chain that walks the audience through your topic makes it easy for your audience to follow and understand your topic.
2. The job of the presenter is to apply the topic to the interest of the audience. Do not leave it up to the audience to try and figure it out.
3. Applying the content to the audience can only happen after you have created the opening and have selected the content to support it.

Successful messages, either sent or received, must be built around a recognizable logic chain to be understood. Our brains demand order, and when we respond to a message, the first thing our minds do is to see if it relates to something we already know. If it does, then we compare what we know to the information presented and determine if it should add to what we already know about the topic.

Writing to Be Spoken and Not to Be Read

Writing for a presentation is different and requires a different kind of writing style. In a presentation, the audience hears the information once as the presenter is delivering it. It goes by the audience at the speed of how the presenter talks. The audience can't stop the presenter and say, "Sorry, I didn't get that. Could you repeat that?" That's why I call writing for a presentation, "Writing that is to be spoken and not to be read."

When we read, we have the option to stop and go back to review the material that we didn't get. In a presentation, the audience hears the material once with no review. The audience either gets it or not. That's why the content must be in a different style, one that is clear and straightforward. The sentences shouldn't contain too many connective pronouns that keep adding ideas.

Figure 7.1 The perfect cup of tea!
Photo: AlexLmx/Getty Images

Too many ideas

The ingredients to make tea are tea, water and sugar, and milk optional in proper amounts blended together in a pot not too big but big enough to hold all the ingredients with room at the top for steam, if it is an electric tea maker then the size isn't an issue because the pot will shut off automatically eliminating any concern about the size of the pot making you free to do something else.

Sentences like the one above will confuse an audience. When an audience hears that many ideas in a single sentence, they will shut down and start their self-talk, ignoring the presenter.

One or two ideas per sentence

The ingredients to make tea are tea, water, sugar, and milk. Blend the ingredients in a pot not too big but big enough to hold all the ingredients with room at the top for steam. If you are using an electric tea maker, then the size isn't an issue because the pot will shut off automatically. It will eliminate any concerns about the size of the container, making you free to do something else.

Sentences containing one or two ideas will lead an audience and give them time to listen and to internalize the concepts. The ideas should build on one another, creating connections leading to your conclusion. *The conclusion should include a restatement of the opening that connects all the ideas, achieving the audience's reaction that you have planned.*

Controlling Your Body Language

One of the common sayings about body language is, "Control it, or it will control you!" The problem with body language is it could be sending a secondary message that contradicts the main message you are trying to send. If a presenter moves too much or does something with their body that distracts the audience, the audience will focus on the distraction and stop listening.

There are many stories of presenters that had lost the audience's attention and didn't know it—those who suddenly did a facial expression at the wrong time or closed their eyes too long or shifted back and forth when they spoke or never looked at the audience. We pick up many clues when we are listening to a presenter or just listening in a conversation.

- We hear not only **what** people are saying but the **tone** of how they are saying it.
- We sense whether the person is relaxed or tense, or if they are distracted by something, and have stopped talking directly to us.

Our senses pick up these clues very quickly, and we react to them without being conscious of why we are feeling the way we do. If you have ever bought a car and watched as the salesperson walked across the showroom floor toward you, before they get to you, you dislike them. You don't know why, but you just don't like them. The salesperson might have done something or walked in a way that reminded you of something you don't like. When the salesperson finally reaches you, they have about 15 or 20 seconds to say or do something that might change your opinion of them.

How to Self-Manage Your Body Language

Eye Contact

The first thing you should do when you are presenting is to make eye contact with the audience. Making eye contact will establish a connection between you and the audience. Eye contact tells the audience you are talking to them and that they should listen. We tend to listen to people who are looking directly at us when they are talking, rather than to people who look away from us. Once you have made a connection to the audience, your body language should support that connection.

Internal Distractions

Our external body language is influenced by our internal thinking when we present. If, for instance, we are judging ourselves when we are presenting, then there is a danger that we will be distracted and make a mistake. It is difficult to do two things at once when you are performing: maintaining the connection with the audience and judging our performance. It can lead to an out-of-body experience where you suddenly make a mistake and then don't know where you are in your presentation.

To control your body language, you must be present with the audience. That means you must concentrate on what you are saying when you are saying it. Don't think about what comes later and don't think about another section in your presentation.

Concentrating on what you are saying when you say it is the secret to controlling your body language. Then, when you present, your body language will be in sync with what you are saying. You shouldn't have to think about your body if you remain present with your audience. After all, we never think of our body language when we are having conversations during the day. We take it for granted that our bodies are in sync with what we are saying. That's because we are concentrating on what we are saying in the conversation and nothing else.

> To control your body language, you must be
> present with the audience.

We are usually totally present in our daily conversations. That immersion in what we are saying is what we should apply to our presentations.

Once you are present with the audience, don't be distracted by any reaction or lack of response from the audience. The time to judge your performance is after you finish your presentation. It is exceedingly difficult to judge your performance while you are performing. No matter how you are doing, no matter what the response of the audience, don't start evaluating how you are doing. It will distract you, and you will lose focus.

> No matter what the response of the audience, don't start evaluating how you are doing.

I remember watching a comic at a club in New York City. He was doing well and getting big laughs from the audience except for a man sitting down front near the stage. The comic saw him and started focusing on the man who wasn't laughing, trying to make him laugh. The man didn't laugh. When the comic came off the stage, he was disappointed. He thought he failed because one guy didn't laugh. The comic said, "I bombed!"

I was astonished. The comic got laughs from 99.9 percent of the audience and still thought he failed. He didn't realize what was happening because he was distracted by one person's reaction and was unable to see the reality of his performance.

> Lesson—Don't evaluate your performance on stage! Wait until you finish your presentation and then look back and evaluate what happened.

Your ability to evaluate a presentation while you are presenting is flawed since you can't do two things at once—present and evaluate. *You will not be able to know what is happening, and you will make the wrong judgments or misread the situation completely.*

Internal feelings during a presentation

When I conduct workshops for presentation and communication coaching, I ask the participants to do a short presentation on anything they choose. During one workshop, a female participant had just finished, and I thought she had done very well. I asked her, "How did you feel when you were presenting?" She said, "I felt nervous, anxious, and my hands were shaking." She assumed she did poorly.

I then asked the other participants who saw her presentation to tell us what they thought of her performance. They responded that they thought she did very well and didn't see any of the nervousness or shaking that she was describing. When she heard that, she was surprised. She began to realize that what she was feeling internally was not being projected externally to the audience. After hearing that, she began to relax.

So, remember, regardless of how you feel internally during a presentation, you can relax in knowing that the audience is probably unaware of how you are feeling. Stay focused on the audience and concentrate on what you are saying.

CHAPTER 8

Presentation Versus Conversation

- Connecting demands interaction.
- It is not a data dump.
- What is the difference?
- Be interactive with the information.
- The value of a story in conversation.
- How do we listen to the information?

Most people learn most of what they know through conversations, informal interactions that people engage in every day. Conversations are the lifeblood of how we gather information and make decisions. If conversations are so important, then why don't we use that style in presentations? Why do presenters insist on talking **to** the audience and not **with** the audience?

Once a connection is made with the audience, we should pull them closer using a conversation. Once we are talking with the audience, then we should involve them in our subject matter. We should design the examples around what the audience knows, something the audience can relate to and understand.

So many times, presenters ignore the audience's needs and do a data dump. They focus on getting as much information out to the audience as they can. They go into detail about everything and drone on and on. Getting lost in the weeds can work for a presenter, but it is the sure way to turn off your audience. Ignoring the audiences' self-interest can be a fatal mistake if you want the audience to listen.

> The difference between a presentation and a conversation is essential in connecting with an audience. A presentation presents content without the consideration of the audience, and a conversation offers content that engages an audience.
>
> Presentations without engagement are monologues. Presentations that are conversations take the audience on a journey through the material, leaving the audience enriched with the content.

The Value of Story in Presentations

Many times, when we are in conversation with someone, we communicate using stories. We tell people what happened, who got caught, what an embarrassing moment we had, what we saw happen to someone else, or the latest gossip in the office. The story is how we receive and give information. It's the one form of communication that everyone recognizes immediately. We've been telling stories for a long time. Even before there was writing, there was an oral tradition of handing down information from one generation to the next through stories. It's in our bones.

Stories make our messages memorable. When you tell a story, people take it with them and transport it to someone else. Our brains react quicker to stories and retain more of the information contained in stories. When we tell or hear a story, it promotes an emotional connection and creates stronger ties between the teller and the listener.

Stories drive our entertainment from TV to films to books to social media. Can you remember how you felt watching your favorite movie or TV show? There's an excitement, an emotional rush that transports us right into the story. We can feel the emotions; our senses relate as if it is happening to us. It feels like a great ride, a roller coaster.

The power of a story is real and can take an audience anywhere you want to take them. It can create awareness, inform, shock, surprise, and amaze. With a story, you can hold the audience in the palm of your hand.

If stories can do all that, why don't more presenters use stories in their presentations?

I believe it's because presenters are focusing on the content and not on the audience. They forget they are talking to people just like themselves, people who are attracted to stories every day. We are awash with stories, and yet we forget to use them in our presentations.

Stories can make your content come alive!

My friend Mary at the dentist

My friend Mary, a very funny person, was sitting in the dentist's chair. Her dentist was about to start a procedure and said, "This is going to be a little uncomfortable." Mary said, "If it hurts, can I have your Mercedes?" The dentist said, "OK, it's going to hurt." Mary said, "Fine, as long as we're clear."

When you are searching for stories, start with experiences and situations in your own life. Many of the things that happen to you will relate to other people. Telling stories that relate to the human condition is an excellent way to connect with your audience.

We are all striving for the same things, like raising our children, working to succeed, or having a successful relationship with our spouses or friends. These are subjects that resonate with an audience.

Take notice of the stories that you like. What was it that kept your interest and made you want to follow the story? An interesting character, a funny situation, a suspenseful moment, and a feeling of overcoming a challenge are the elements of stories. If they captured you, they would undoubtedly capture someone else.

Stories—the communication lifeline that connects us all

CHAPTER 9

The Art of Presenting

Like any art, presenting must be practiced. It always amazes me when people don't practice or prepare a presentation and then are surprised when it doesn't go well. How can you expect a successful result when you didn't do anything to achieve that result?

Yet people spend time practicing a sport or playing an instrument because they know the only way to get better is to practice. If you play tennis, you can't have a good backhand unless you practice so much that you create a "body habit." So, when you use your backhand, you don't think about where your feet are or how your hands are holding the racket. You simply swing the racket. If you play golf, you must practice your swing off the tee and your putting to be a good golfer.

Asking to join your golf foursome
What if I showed up where you are playing golf with your friends and asked to join your foursome? You would look at me and see I don't have any golf clubs. You would ask me, "Tom, where are your clubs?" I'd say, "I don't have any clubs, but you can lend me yours, right?" You'd then ask me, "Have you ever played golf?" I'd say, "No, but I read a book on golf once." Would you let me join your foursome? Of course not, I don't have the right tools, and I have no experience, and yet I expect to play golf. You would know right away that my expectations are wrong, and it would be a disaster.

Expecting to be good at something when there has been no preparation or practice is wishful thinking. Yet some presenters believe they can be good at presenting even though they haven't worked or prepared anything. They rely on instinct and believe in the moment of performing they will be fine. They never make the connection between being good and practice. When their presentations fail, they blame the audience or other people.

Figure 9.1 Practicing so he can forget it!
Photo: Gilaxia/Getty Images

> How many hours of practice does it take for a musician to know a piece of music so they can forget it and perform the music?

To be good at anything, you *must practice* until it becomes *second nature to you,* and you no longer think about it. *You just do it. It becomes a body habit. It flows.* Look at the top performers in any field, and you will find that their success is not by accident; rather, it is designed through hours of practice.

> How many bats does a minor league professional baseball player have to have before he can move up to the majors? He must have a minimum of a thousand bats or more before he can be eligible to move up. Why? The team wants to be sure the player has seen every pitch in every combination possible so the player can be prepared for major league pitching.

If you want to be a successful presenter, and it isn't just a wish but a strong desire, then practice until you know your presentations so well, you can forget the details and perform them. Knowing your presentation will free you from mentally reviewing your performance over and over. It will relax you and enable you to be present with the audience. Knowing your presentation will give you the confidence to start with conviction and purpose. Presentations are not intellectual exercises. *They are visceral experiences, bringing together your mind, body, and voice.*

CHAPTER 10

Finding Your Style— Discovering Your Comfort Zone

- What is a comfort zone?
- How to define your style
- Your comfort zone and voice
- Resources for your perceptions

What Is a Comfort Zone?

A presentation comfort zone is a feeling inside you where you feel at ease and relaxed to do your presentation. Your comfort zone can be found in your personality. Some people refer to it as your genuine yourself, but I like to describe it as a projection of who you believe you are. It is the way you see the world and how you project yourself in everyday conversations. Your unique way of interacting with the world. What you believe to be important.

If you are in your comfort zone when you present, then you are projecting your genuine self and not acting or pretending to be someone else. Some presenters believe they must assume a different personality when they present. They feel they must be the "expert" or the "model," or someone perfect. Most people cannot act. They haven't been trained in the skills acting and don't know how to be someone else. So, don't try. It will distract you and put you in an uncomfortable mode when you present.

Audiences read *genuineness by the way presenters talk, the sound of their voice, and their body language.* I'm sure you have been in an audience

Figure 10.1 *Connecting is easy when you know your audience!*
Photo: mapodile/Getty Images

watching a presenter and felt that you liked them; you didn't examine it, you just felt it. That's the feeling and connection you want from your audiences when you present.

I work with clients and help them create their own "comfort zone." It is essential to become aware of who we are. How you perceive the world and how you communicate that perception to others. Your impressions of the world are important because they are unique to you. No one else sees the world exactly as you do. I often ask my clients, "*What is your competitive edge*"? They reply, "The depth of their companies or their organizations." I then say, "*No, it's you! You are the competitive edge because no one is exactly like you.* How you see the world and how you communicate your vision and passion is your competitive edge. *You are unique!*"

You are the competitive edge. No one is exactly like you. You are unique!

They are usually surprised because they have never thought of themselves as being unique. We tell our uniqueness through the stories we tell. Tell them what you see, hear, and observe, and they will connect with you.

How to Define Your Style.
Your Perceptions of the World

Your style is the way you present yourself to other people. How people perceive you. Our style defines us and can help people remember us. When defining a client's style, I ask them to answer a few questions.

Questions About Your Style

- What type of business personality are you? Detail-oriented?
- Are you motivated by ideas more than facts? Always aware of the bigger picture? A visionary?
- What do you think your presentation style is: formal or informal?
- How do you think other people see you?

These questions can help you define your style and your personality. They can help you become aware of how other people see you. These questions can also help you see if your internal perception of your self matches the external perception that people have of you. Many times, people believe what they feel internally is projected externally. That is not always true.

We are not as transparent as we think. When you believe you have defined your style, ask someone who knows you, and you trust to verify your style. Ask them to tell you what your style is when you present. See if they agree with your assessment. If they do agree, then you have successfully defined your style. If they don't agree, then record yourself and try to see what others see.

Your Comfort Zone and Voice

Knowing your style can help you understand how you naturally like to present. It's the way we act in everyday conversations. We don't think about what we are doing in conversations. We just engage people and talk. Bringing that naturalness to your presentation will relax you and allow you to be yourself. Being yourself, when you present, will allow you to relax in front of an audience and create a "comfort zone," allowing people to see you, as you are. This will create a human connection with your audience because they will be able to see themselves. Being in your *comfort zone* will also help you find your *voice*. Your voice is your brand. It's what makes you different from everyone else.

Comics will tell you that the hardest part of being a comic is finding their voice. A comic's voice represents the way they see the world. Once they find it, their comedy is branded to them. All the funny things they do become known as their style of comedy. That's how we tell comics and comedians apart. That's how they build a following. Think of a comic or a comedian you like and see if you can describe how they see the world. Are they angry or overwhelmed about the world or confused as to what happens to them? That's their voice, and it is uniquely tied to them.

When we found our comedy voice

At the end of our performing career, Deanie and I finally found our comedy voice. We were opening a new club in Philadelphia and decided not to do sketches or improvisation. Instead, we decided to talk about our relationship and our kids. Our oldest, Michael, was five years old at the time and was a super fan of the "Blues Brothers" movie with John Belushi and Dan Ackroyd. There was a scene in it that he loved in which the Blues Brothers were escaping from the police. Just before they took off, Dan Ackroyd and John Belushi would check what they had. Our son demanded that he wouldn't go to nursery school unless we acted out the scene from the movie. So, before we could take him to nursery school, I did the scene with him. So, we would be in the car, and he would say, "Daddy do it." So I'd have to say, "it's 106 miles to Chicago, we got a full tank of gas, a half a pack of cigarettes, it's dark, and we're wearing sunglasses." And he would say, "Hit it!" Then I could take him to nursery school.

That was the first time we told the audience about who we were and our family. The audience loved it and wanted to hear more about us. After playing hundreds of characters on stage and TV, we discovered that what the audience wanted to hear was who we were and how we interacted with our son. It seems so obvious, yet it took us a long time to know that.

Resources for Your Perceptions

Once you have your *comfort zone and your voice*, then it's time to demonstrate your unique perception of the world. To do that, incorporate stories, observations, and comments about how you see the world, into your presentations.

You can use examples from your favorite movies, TV shows, books, or even examples of the stories from your family, as we did in the act. They can be great resources for developing your unique perception of the world. Another source for your stories can be the passion you bring to your job and why you are proud of what you do. I often ask my architecture clients, to develop a design story for their clients, showing them how they decided what to keep and what not to use in developing the best design. The design story lets the client in on how the creative process works and how the architect understands the client's needs.

> Being in your comfort zone when you present will relax you and help you project your genuine self to the audience.

Talking about your perceptions and letting people in on who you are will make you appear vulnerable to an audience. Showing vulnerability is the way to give something to an audience before you ask for something from them. Being vulnerable will make you seem approachable and friendly.

CHAPTER 11

The Importance of Your Voice

- The sound of your voice.
- How to use your diaphragm; the proper way to breathe.
- A strong voice can create credibility.
- The voice affects the way messages are received.
- How to slow down, if you speak too fast.

The Sound of Your Own Voice

Whenever I video-record a client in a private session and play it back, I always get the same response: "That doesn't sound like me! It sounds too thin and high."

Why is there such a difference between what we sound like internally to what we hear when we are recorded? In our heads, our voices sound full and have a bass sound to it. One of the reasons we sound better in our heads is that our voice reverberates in our skulls. Internally we hear the full richness of our voice, but when we speak, it is the sound of our voice without the effect of our skulls.

The voice to an actor is an instrument: a tool to be used to create characters and communicate feelings and emotions. Actors spend a lifetime developing their instrument, and when we hear a professional actor's voice, we can immediately understand the feelings they are communicating.

One of the things an actor or a singer uses in developing their voices is their diaphragm. Our diaphragms are located just below our belly buttons and expand and contract when we need air to support our voices. Your diaphragm is a crucial tool in developing a good-sounding voice when you present. Like an actor and singer, your diaphragm will enable you to fill a room with a sound that is full and demands attention.

Figure 11.1 *Successful presentations include a presentation voice!*
Photo: Slphotography/Getty Images

How to Use Your Diaphragm

Diaphragm exercise

If you want to test whether you use your diaphragm when you present, here is a simple way. Put your hand on your throat and talk the way you normally do. You should feel a vibration in your throat as you speak. Let's call that your *conversation voice*. Now put both hands just below your belly button. Take a deep breath so you can feel this area as it fills with air.

Now, as you exhale, push in with both hands, and you should feel air coming from your diaphragm. Repeat this and this time say "Oh" as you exhale. What you hear is your voice being supported by your diaphragm. Let's call this your *presentation voice*. Repeat the exercise one more time, and this time, see how long you can sustain the sound of "Oh" before you run out of breath. The longer you can sustain the sound of "Oh," the more you are using your diaphragm. See if you can sustain the sound for at least 5 to 10 seconds. Repeat this exercise about five or six times so you can tell the difference between *your conversation voice and your presentation voice*. It can help to record this exercise, so that you can hear the difference.

A Strong Voice Can Create Credibility

Creating your presentation voice by using your diaphragm, will make your voice seem fuller and give it more body when you present. It will make you appear more confident and knowledgeable about your topic. A strong voice enables you to take control of the space when you present.

Audiences are drawn to strong voices and feel that the speaker is in control. Your voice, along with your body, is the first thing an audience relates to when you approach them. Audiences make quick decisions, usually in the first 20 to 45 seconds of a presentation, as to whether they are going to listen to a presenter. Having a strong voice will make it easier for an audience to listen and then to connect with you.

> Your voice is an essential element of a successful message.

The Voice Affects the Way Messages Are Received

Developing a presentation voice can give you command of an audience and allow you to transport them into your presentation. Your presentation voice can bring color and meaning to your presentation, allowing the audience to experience your presentation in a memorable way.

You can also use a presentation voice in a meeting. It won't be as loud as when you present to a group, but it will project confidence and control when you respond or when you give a report.

A client takes control
A client was giving reports about her department to the board of directors. She felt intimidated and was afraid she was going to make a mistake. We did a personality and subject profile of the board and was able to identify the areas of each board member to prepare for their questions. She started to realize that she had control of her presentation. Next, we examined her voice and discovered that she used her conversation voice when she presented. She started doing the exercises for using her diaphragm when she spoke. Slowly, she started to develop a presentation voice that was fuller and stronger when she spoke. She continued to practice and

developed a strong presentation voice. At the board meeting she delivered her department's report and answered all the questions of the board. After the meeting, she told me that for the first time, she felt in control and relaxed. She also said that when she spoke, everyone on the board looked at her and not at their computers.

> Use your diaphragm to create a presentation voice and take control of the space.

Speaking too fast

If you talk too quickly when you present, then here's a tip that might help.

When I directed voiceover talent for a commercial, I would hand them the script to read. While reading the text, the voiceover talent would add slash lines (/) to the copy. They did this to identify the ideas and mark where they should take a breath. They wanted to sustain their breath for a complete thought and then stop and take a breath. By taking breaths after completed ideas, they were able to communicate the concepts one at a time. It slowed down their read and gave time to the listener to internalize the message.

So the next time you are practicing for a presentation, try marking your copy for complete thoughts with a slash to show where you should take a breath. Taking breaths will slow you down and give your audience a chance to hear your presentation.

CHAPTER 12

Speaker Support—Making Your Messages Easier to Understand

- To use slides or not to use slides, that is the question.
- Effective slides are visual.
- Best practices for PowerPoint slides.

To Use Slides or Not to Use Slides, That Is the Question

Successful messages are easily understood and show relationships between ideas. They move an audience from one idea to another in a seamless way, pulling them further and further into the presentation, making the audience wanting to hear more and more. Anything that interrupts that flow should not be used.

Answering the question of using slides or not is simple. Do you need something to enhance your ideas and make your content more compelling? Then slides are good to use. Slides are a good tool to use in a presentation, but if they are used to an extreme, they can dominate a presentation and kill a good presentation.

Effective Slides Are Visual

Slides can help your audience understand your message. They should never be "The Message" and should not be the focus of your presentation. When you turn your back to the audience and talk directly to the slides, you are disconnecting from your audience. PowerPoint and other graphic programs are fine for giving meaning to an idea or by showing its application or comparison to something else but should never be the focus of your presentation.

*"I'll pause for a moment so you can
let this information sink in."*

Figure 12.1 Slides should always be easy to read!
Cartoon: Gahan Wilson/Cartoon Stock

Don't use your slide deck as a prompt for the presentation. Use a
Talk Track to remember the content of your presentation. A *Talk Track* is
a logical chain of thought that connects the ideas in your presentation.
It's how you are going to present the flow of ideas in your presentation.
A *Talk Track* is more reliable in recalling the order of your presentation.
It gives you more flexibility if you must change the presentation quickly.
Slides cannot be changed during a presentation. Your *Talk Track* is more
important than any slide.

A Talk Track consists of the first idea—transition to the second idea—
transition to the third idea—then transition to the fourth idea, and so on.

Design your slides after you have created the *Talk Track*. The logic chain of the *Talk Track* will help you to decide where the slides ought to go in the presentation. It can highlight the sections and ideas that need more clarity. Think of the slides as visual aids in helping the audience comprehend and apply the ideas. They are also an opportunity to compare the content to information that the audience already knows, demonstrating that you know the understanding level and self-interest of the audience.

Best Practices for Slides

- Background color should make your slides easy to see and read.
- Slides should be simple and not complex.
- If you use data tables, be sure they are easy to read.
- Diagrams shouldn't look like piping systems.
- Use short phrases and not sentences or paragraphs.
- The less type, the better.
- Fonts sizes for slides should be 18pt or greater.
- Do not use clip art. Instead, use pictures that relate to your subject.
- In general, use as few slides as possible.

Following these simple guidelines will help you create slides that will enhance your message and allow you to magnify your theme. Slides can also add an entertainment factor to your presentations.

CHAPTER 13

Preparing for a Webcast, Broadcast, or a Recorded Presentation

- How are online and recorded video presentations different?
- How to use a teleprompter.
- Recording your practice.

How Are Webcast and Recorded Presentations Different?

Recorded and webcast presentations are different from live performances due to what the audience sees or doesn't see. As a presenter, you should be aware of how the various technologies like live-streaming and recorded presentations treat your messages. You should know how the audience is receiving your image and voice. Knowing some basics can help you manage your presentations on these mediums.

When we watch presentations on our phones or other mobile devices, we usually look at the center of the screen since those screens are small. Even when we watch TV, your eyes are usually looking at the center of the screen. The reason we look at the center of the screen is that our eyes can take in all the information at once. We don't have to scan or move our eyes around the screen to see what is happening. Even if the screen is large, like a TV screen that is 60 inches or more, we still tend to look at the center of the screen.

Since our eyes do not have to move to see all the information, there is a tendency to get bored with the images because we see all the information

Figure 13.1 *Connecting on camera is just as important as connecting in person!*
Photo: Azmani/Getty Images

so quickly. To create interest, you will notice that the images on these small screens change very rapidly. This keeps our attention since the new stimulus is being presented every one to two seconds. Commercials are a particularly good example of this technique.

In comparison, when we watch a movie in a theater, the screen is large 70 mm or Imax size; it forces us to scan the entire screen to get all the information. However, movie makers still try to keep all the vital material in the center of the screen since they know that's where the audience tends to look.

Knowing where the audience is looking is essential when you design your presentations and slides for recorded or online presentations. Animation, if available, works because it creates a separate moment for the viewers. Slides should contain movement like builds, elements added to a slide one at a time, to make ideas easier to understand. They should be easy to follow since the viewers only see them when they are on camera.

The second factor to consider when you are presenting online or recorded is that when you are talking, the viewers will be focusing on your eyes. That's why it is important to look directly into the camera and be present. Remember *being present* means concentrating on what you are saying when you say it. On phones, tablets, and computers, there is a

Figure 13.2 To connect on camera, look directly into the camera!
Photo: AJ_Watt/Getty Images

tendency to look at the other person and not directly into your camera. It is hard getting used to it, but looking at the camera will give the appearance that you are looking directly at the viewer.

Using a Teleprompter

The next thing to consider is whether you are using a teleprompter. A teleprompter is a device that fits over the camera's lenses. It enables the presenter to see words in front of the lenses that the viewers don't see. Teleprompters can be used in front of the lenses or as glass screens on either side of a podium. Speakers can read their speeches by looking back and forth between screens. A script is prepared and projected through the teleprompter, so that the presenter can read the presentation.

The prompter operator moves the words according to the speed of the reading of the presenter. The trick to reading teleprompter is to read complete phrases before you take a breath. In that way, you can give yourself time for expression and hear what you are reading. Reading a teleprompter is a skill and takes practice. So, if you have time, practice reading from the prompter and it will go smoother when you are on camera.

What if you are not using a teleprompter, then how do you remember your presentation? Your *Talk Track*, which is the logical outline of how you are transitioning from one idea to another, will help in this situation. The *Talk Track* will create an informal conversation with the viewers. It will also help in projecting yourself since you won't be reading from a teleprompter.

Once you have internalized your content for a recorded or live online presentation, the next step is to practice your presentation by recording yourself. You can use your phone or any other device that has recording capabilities.

Recording Your Practice

When you record yourself, start by taking a deep breath, let it out, then take a small step forward toward the recording device, smile, and begin to talk. The deep breath will relax you, and the small step will create movement and put you in preparation. Finally, the smile will relax your facial muscles and make you look welcoming.

When you look at the playback of your practices, remember to be kind to yourself. The audience sees you as a full human being and not any flaws you think you have visually. The audience will be thinking about themselves and not judging you as you perform. In your recorded practices, look for anything that might distract your viewers from your eyes and face. *If you are present when you perform, your body language and voice will be in sync and display a single message.*

Things to remember when doing webcast and recorded presentations:

- Viewers see less of you than in a live performance.
- Viewers look at the center of the screen.
- When reading from a teleprompter, read complete phrases or ideas, then take a breath.
- While talking to the camera, look directly into the camera.
- Practice by recording yourself.
- Be kind to yourself when you see the playback of your practice.

CHAPTER 14

Presenting at a Business Meeting

- What's wrong with meetings today?
- How to re-create the employee meeting.
- Questions to ask when preparing a meeting.
- Tips to increase participants' interest and attention.

How many times have you sat in a meeting and said to yourself, "What am I doing here? I have a thousand things to do, and this meeting is a waste of time." Meetings can consume our business lives and kill productivity. Yet meetings don't have to be that way. We should treat meetings as if they were presentations and speak to the self-interest of those attending.

"Slap me when he's done. I'm putting myself into a self-induced coma."

Figure 14.1 *People are only human!*
Cartoon: Chris Wildt/Cartoon Stock

Those who conduct or present in a meeting should use the same techniques that apply to a presentation. We should treat meetings as if they were presentations and speak to the self-interest of those attending. What do they expect from the meeting? Why should they listen?

Most meetings are not well planned and tend to become routine and predictable. They create a template that everyone knows, and no one wants to change. Many times, they begin with the specifics of a topic rather than beginning with the conclusion and then showing the details. It's like watching a bad movie repeatedly. You know what's coming and you know it's going to be bad.

How to revive meetings before they become predictable? In my experience in coaching meetings, the structures should be blown up every six months. That seems to be the time limit before participants get bored.

Re-Creating the Employee Meeting

When I was coaching an architectural firm on how to conduct their monthly employee meeting, I discovered that the principals of the firm were leading the sessions of the firm were conducting the meetings. They were concerned because they were not getting good feedback and the participation was dropping. When I asked who was preparing the content for the meeting, they said that the principals were doing it without input from the employees.

I told them that although they called it an employee meeting, it was a meeting for the principals to tell the employees what they wanted and not about employee needs. I asked them to send out an e-mail asking what some of the concerns were that the employees wanted to discuss in the meeting. When the responses came back, we compared them to the topics the principals had prepared. To their surprise, nothing matched the principals' lists of concerns. They saw for the first time that the concerns of the employees were not their concerns and that many of the principals were not even aware of the employees' interests.

The principals realized that if they wanted to increase participation and really have an employee meeting, they would have to change the structure and delivery of the meeting. They would have to let the employees design and deliver the meeting with the principals being facilitators.

Getting out of the way and letting the participants design the meeting is not easy. It feels counterintuitive. As principals, they felt they had to take charge and lead the meeting. If a meeting is essential and it should be, then the design and the topics should speak to the self-interest of the participants.

That brings up another question. How much is the difference between sending an e-mail and having a meeting? An hour or two of wasted time. If the topic of a meeting can be handled in an e-mail, then it should be. If there are only two to five items that can be handled in an e-mail, then they should be. If the subject matter can be explained on a page or two, then it's an e-mail. This difference is important to consider if meetings are going to have value and represent time well spent.

Questions to ask when preparing a meeting:

- What is the purpose of the meeting?
- If there isn't a reason to meet, then why meet?
- If the reason for the meeting is to deliver new information about a product or service, then ask:
  - Why is essential for the participants to know?
  - How will the information help them?
  - How will the subject matter make their jobs easier or enhance what they are doing?

- If the meeting's purpose is to review information or material, then ask:
  - Has anything changed since we last reviewed the material?
  - Has performance lacked by not implementing the information or material?

- If the meeting's purpose is to evaluate performance, then ask:
  - Is it a positive or negative message?
  - If it is a negative message, then how can the meeting begin with a positive statement about performance?

○ Is there a visual or a video to introduce or summarize the topic of the meeting?

Tips to increase participants' interest and attention

- Start with an opening that explains the value of the content to the participants.
- Tell them how they will benefit from the information.
- Tell them how the information will help in doing their jobs.

Answering these questions will position the self-interest of the participants right at the start and give a reason why they should listen. Ask for input from the participants. If the number of participants is small, ask them for their suggestions to make the meetings better. If the number of participants is large, create a brief questionnaire, no more than five questions, that you can e-mail asking for their responses. Incorporate the suggestions into the next meeting. If the meeting is a review for employees and is about topics that directly affect their work, become a facilitator. Let the participants run the meeting. *Let them organize topics and agendas for the meeting.*

Steps to improve meetings:

- Let the participants design the meeting.
- Let the participants create the structure of the meeting.
- Allow them to decide who should present and what topics should be covered.
- Once everyone agrees, facilitate the meeting.

> Allowing the participants to create the content of a meeting will ensure their interest and attention.

Meetings can become an essential tool again if we treat them as a necessity for communicating information that we can only deliver in person. How else can people be heard and have input into the complex problems facing businesses today?

> It isn't the number of meetings but the quality of the sessions that can revive the creativity and collaboration of a company.

CHAPTER 15

Using Humor in Presentations

Guidelines for Using Humor

- Do you have the right to laugh?
- If you are not a member of the group you are going to make fun of, then you must get permission from the group to do it.
- Make humor a seamless part of the presentation.
- You can't make fun of someone else's beliefs or what they consider to be sacred.
- It is always appropriate to make fun of yourself.

In today's world, we must be aware not to offend an individual or group when we use humor in presentations. We all have heard stories or read accounts of performers and presenters making a joke, a reference, or a comment that offends an individual or group.

Even though these are sensitive times, the use of humor in a presentation can still be powerful. Humor can magnify a message and make it memorable. When people laugh, it is a sign that they understand what we are saying and will remember it. It's shorthand for saying we follow and relate to what you are saying.

In medieval times, the only one who could talk truth to the king without getting his head chopped off was the jester or the fool. That's because the jester used humor to convey his message to the king. As the saying goes, much truth is told to power using humor!

Figure 15.1 One size does not fit all when it comes to using humor!
Photo: trangiap/Getty Images

How to Use Humor in a Presentation

Some would say, "Very Carefully."

Here are some humor guidelines that will help you to determine whether or not you should use humor in a presentation. These guidelines were developed when I taught a course at the University of Pennsylvania in Organizational Dynamics Master program. The course was "Humor in Organizations or How to Get What You Want." As a reminder, these are guidelines and not rules.

Do You Have the Right to Laugh?

The right to laugh means, "Are you a member of the group you are about to make fun of?" If you are, then you have the right to laugh. If you are not, then you can't make fun of the group because you are not a member.

If you are Italian, then you can make an Italian joke or comment about Italians, Jews can make fun of Jews, Irish can make fun of the Irish, English people can make fun of the English, and so on.

If you are not a member of the group you are going to make fun of, then you must get permission from the group before you do it.

The only way you can say something humorous about a group you don't belong to is to have permission from the group. You get consent by asking if what you are going to say is offensive to the members of that group. Before you make fun, be sure you have permission and are confident that your remarks will not offend the group.

Make sure the humor is part of your presentation seamlessly.

Don't make your humor stand out by saying, "Here's a joke" or "Here's something funny." Never telegraph that you are about to use humor. Instead, embed in your presentation, so if it doesn't work, you can move on and won't have to feel naked in front of your audience when you don't get the laugh.

You can't make fun of someone else's belief or what they consider to be sacred.

I believe there are boundaries when it comes to humor. If the comment or joke is making fun of another person's sacredness, then you will never get a laugh from that group or person. All of us have ideas or beliefs that we consider sacred. It is those things we hold dear and believe they are not subject to humor or ridicule.

A lesson learned, the hard way

As a young comic, I was booked to perform for a religious group. At the time, I didn't check out the group or thought about what the group considered sacred. I was going to entertain. In my act at the time, I had bible stories in which I portrayed the characters as not being too bright. So, I went into one of my bible stories, and in the middle of my performance, a woman stood up and announced, "We will have no more of that!" I was stunned and, for a moment, didn't know what to say. I thanked the woman and went on to other material and left the stage as soon as I could. I had made fun of the audience's sacredness and ruined the performance. As a young comic, I had not only broken one of the guidelines, but I didn't know the audience and had made no attempt to find out who they were.

So, the next time you want to use humor, be sure to check out the guidelines and don't make fun of someone else's sacredness.

Humor Guidelines

It is always appropriate to make fun of yourself.

Highlighting how you interact with the world or doing stupid things we all do is a safe way to use humor. Make sure your comment relates to your topic and applies to the human condition. Comics do it all the time by talking about their families, their kids, their love life, and anything else in their lives.

What to do when a joke doesn't work.

When I was in comedy, and a joke wasn't working, I would always check the premise and not the punch line.

All jokes start with a premise or a set up that explains the conditions of the joke.

A guy walks into a bar with a duck on his head. He goes up to the bartender, and the duck says, "Hey buddy, how can I get this guy off my ass." In this example, the audience has to know a bar, a duck, and a bartender. If they didn't know any or only one of the references, then the joke wouldn't work. My kids used to laugh because they never expected the duck to talk.

So be sure your audience understands the references you use. It becomes important if there are cultural differences between you and your audience. Or if you are talking to a culture completely different from your own. Research who you are presenting to and find out as much as you can about them. It will help you connect to your audience.

> Humor is a powerful tool and can make your presentation memorable, but be careful how you use it!

CHAPTER 16

Managing All the Elements

- Bringing it all together
- Developing a performance stance
- How to get and handle feedback
- Fail-safe presentations

Bringing It All Together

Now that you know who your audience is and created an opening. You've prepared the content to support your opening, and then practiced by putting your presentation on its feet, and then successfully internalized your presentation. It's time to *forget it!*. That's right, *forget it*. Sounds strange? It isn't.

Forgetting it means that you are present when you perform your presentation.

You concentrate on the audience and on what you are saying when you say it. You are not talking internally to yourself, and you are not thinking ahead or focusing on how the audience is receiving you. Remember, a musician practices a piece of music until they can internalize the music. So, when they perform, they don't think about the notes or where to put their hands. They have created a body habit that takes over when they play. They are free to be in the moment and to be one with the audience.

Forgetting it also means trusting in yourself to know what you want to say once you get there. Remember, you do it every day in conversation. You let one idea flow into another, and don't worry about what you are going to say next. When you talk to a person in a conversation, you improvise what you are going to say next according to the subject matter of your discussion.

That's the goal of presenting—creating a conversation with the audience. Your ideas are the vehicle that can take your audience anywhere you want to take them.

Developing a Performance Stance

A *performance stance* is a way a person physically presents themselves each time they present. It's the way they stand, the sound of their voice, and the way they immediately connect with the audience. It allows a presenter to think about the audience and not about themselves.

You'll notice that when you watch your favorite comedienne, they stand and move around the stage in a very deliberate way. Their *performance stance* relaxes them and adds to their style. Once you develop your own, it will do the same for you.

To develop your *performance stance*, start by standing in front of a mirror. Stand straight, don't slough, and be sure you're standing on both feet. Be aware of how it feels. You should feel relaxed and not stiff. Your head should be up and your arms by your side, relaxed. Standing straight and looking directly at the audience signals you are ready to begin.

When you talk, you should use your presentation voice, supported by your diaphragm. Your *presentation voice* should fill the space, project confidence, and demand attention from the audience. Your presentation voice will add to your performance stance.

Smile before you begin to talk-not a broad smile but a pleasant one that says welcome.

Smiling relaxes your facial muscles and relieves some of the tension when you begin. So many presenters forget to smile, and yet it is the easiest thing to do to show you are likable and open to connect to the audience.

Once you have developed your *performance stance*, it will be the body habit that you will use every time you present. It will become your ritual for preparing to perform and focus your energy on the audience, so you can be mindful and present.

Your performance stance can be helpful even if you're not presenting but participating in a meeting. If you are sitting at a conference table for a meeting, sit up, elbows on the table, and use your presentation voice when you talk. Elbows on the table will prevent you from swinging back and forth in your chair when you speak. Your voice and body are powerful tools when you communicate and will display confidence and credibility when you talk.

> Your voice and body language are powerful tools.
> Use them to your advantage.

How to Get and Handle Feedback

Feedback is essential if presenters want to improve. Many presenters are afraid of feedback. They view it as criticism or rejection. Knowing how we are perceived is critical if we are going to know what to improve. The secret to feedback is to ask trusted people who don't have an agenda in giving feedback. They could be co-workers, friends, and family. The main thing is that they will be honest in their comments and have a desire to help.

Asking for Feedback

When you ask for feedback, be sure to ask for specific things you want the person to consider. For example:

- Were your ideas clear?
- Could they hear you?
- Did they understand your slides at first glance?

Asking for specific things you want them to look for will direct them and give them a purpose for the feedback. If you don't give them specific items to look for, then they will tend to offer things like rewriting your presentation or telling you how you should deliver your presentation. Directing the feedback to specific items you are concerned about will help in improving the presentation.

Another way of getting feedback is to do an audience survey. Polling the audience is an excellent way to get feedback on whether your message was received and perceived.

When creating questions, select ones on a sliding scale—a scale, for instance, from not very well to exceptionally well or (1) strongly agree and (5) strongly disagree.

Questions should be direct and easy to understand.

- Was the presentation and subject matter understood, and did it have value for the audience?
- Was the subject matter interesting, and did it meet the expectations of the audience?
- Would they recommend the presentation to another?

Do not include too many questions. Surveys should be short. They should take no longer than five to six minutes to complete. Audience members are in a hurry and don't want to spend a lot of time filling out surveys.

When you get feedback, don't take it personally. You want to remain objective and judge if the input can help you improve your presentation.

There are two kinds of feedback: content and performance. *Content* is easy to deal with since it is about the clarity of your message. Improving your message by using better examples, videos, charts, or stories can make you a better presenter. The feedback can help you pinpoint where the content isn't clear or where the connections of ideas fail to show the audience the transition from one idea to another.

Performance feedback can be harder to receive because it is about your body language or your voice. If there is something that you're doing that is distracting the audience from your message, you should want to know about it. The next time you present, you could ask a friend to record you from the audience so you can evaluate your performance. Remember to correct your body language; make sure you are present and only focusing on what you are saying when you say it.

Don't be afraid of silence. Silence or looking at the audience and not speaking can help with nervous ticks or internal thinking when you disconnect from an audience. Silence can also slow down the tendency to fill the space with talking.

Remember using a performance voice can help with most concerns about being heard. Even if you use a microphone, it is better to use a performance voice when you present. A performance voice can add color and expression to your message and command attention from the audience. A performance voice can also help calm your body language. Using the diaphragm enables you to take larger breaths when you speak, thus relaxing your muscles.

Fail-Safe Presentations

Fail-safe presentations mean you have control of the content, the delivery, and the stage.

Having control of these elements will allow you to be free to focus on the audience and to be aware if something unexpected were to happen. Even if something does happen, you still have your talk track and can continue your message. The good performers try to incorporate whatever happens into their performance.

Going with the flow

To end our act, when I was a performer, I did a pantomime about a guy who had just broken up with his girlfriend and wanted to die. We called it "*The Suicide.*"

It began with me pantomiming, walking into a room, and being very depressed. Our piano player would play a sad blues song. When I looked and hugged the picture of my girlfriend, he would play *As Time Goes By* from the film *Casablanca. Since* I was so broken-hearted, I decided to kill myself, but everything I tried didn't work. I tried hanging, but the rope broke; I tried a knife, but it was rubber; I tried shooting myself, but there were no bullets. Finally, I took sleeping pills. Suddenly the phone rang, and it was my girlfriend who wanted to come back; the piano played *As Time Goes By. I w*as overjoyed and hung up.

Suddenly I look at the audience, and the piano player played the blues. I realized that I had taken sleeping pills and started to yawn. I didn't want to die. My girlfriend was coming back! I started to hit myself in the face trying to stay awake but to no avail. As the lights slowly go out, I continued to slap myself in the face trying to stay awake.

One night while performing this pantomime in New York City, a woman in the audience suddenly started describing everything I was doing on stage. She says, "Look, he's sad, he's trying to kill himself. The rope broke, the knife was rubber." She didn't realize or cared that I and the entire audience could hear her. So, to let her know that I could hear her, I went to the front of the stage and pantomime a window and then pantomimed shutting it. As I finished closing the window; I heard the lady's voice ring out, "Look, he's closing the window!" She continued narrating my pantomime until it was over.

Sometimes it's better to go along with whatever happens. The audience liked the pantomime, and the response was the best we had ever gotten for the piece. It taught us that when the unexpected happens, don't fight it but incorporate it into what you're doing. The audience participated during the moment and felt closer and more connected to us.

Figure 16.1 Audience participation can be fun!
Photo: PeopleImages/Getty Images

Making the audience part of what you are doing is the best way to have a fail-safe presentation. Many presenters tend to relax more, knowing they can use what happens to have a deeper connection with the audience. It relieves some of the fear and anxiety that comes with presenting.

Techniques, skills, and management ideas contained in this book will put the control of your presentations in your hands. As a presenter, you will find that control will enable you to custom design a presentation for any audience.

Connecting with your audience is not magic. It shouldn't be something that happens now and then. It should happen every time you present, making your presentations successful every time you present.

So, start experiencing the excitement and fun of knowing that the next time you present it will be exciting and enjoyable for both you and your audience.

Go present and connect!

Reviews and Testimonials

Reading Tom Guggino's book produces an amazing paradigm shift for most people who think they understand how to give a presentation. Whether presenting for sales, marketing, education, professional work or to convince friends and colleagues to pay attention to an issue of importance, this book should be your guide.

> Larry M. Starr, PhD,
> Director, Doctoral Program in
> Strategic Leadership and in
> Complex Systems Leadership,
> Thomas Jefferson University.

"Regardless of your experience or the type of presentation you may deliver, *Present! Connect!* is packed with practical tips to help you connect with your audience and deliver engaging messages. With his "Presentation Process" as a backdrop, Tom leverages his experience as a stand-up comic and professional coach to describe how to deliver high-impact presentations. *Present! Connect!* is a must-read for anyone wanting to learn how to better connect with their audience, create a compelling message, become cognizant of body language and its impact, or project a strong presentation voice."

> Mark Saddic, M.Ed.
> Director, Learning and
> Organizational Effectiveness
> CCI Consulting

Testimonials from Clients

"Tom is an excellent speaking coach and a masterful facilitator for business strategies. I have really enjoyed working with him."

> David Hatton, AIA
> Principal
> Hord Copland Macht

"Tom Guggino has been a tremendous resource to our leadership team during our last three annual strategic planning sessions. His interpersonal skills, emotional intelligence and understanding of organizational dynamics allow him a great platform from which to work effectively across diverse personalities and agendas. He brings practical guidance that is informed by business context, leadership's vision, and the internal and external environment. Always professional, cordial, and thoughtful, working with Tom has been a highly productive, value added learning experience."

Anton Germishuizen
Senior Vice President, BuildingsStantec
Anton Germishuizen Senior Vice President,
Business Leader, Buildings

About the Author

Tom Guggino is a presentation and communications coach on the faculty at Jefferson University in the Doctor of Management in Strategic Leadership program. He has taught and lectured in the graduate programs at the University of Pennsylvania and LaSalle University.

Tom's career began as a comic in the comedy team called McAndrews and Gino that performed sketches and improvisation. Their credits include CBS television, clubs on both the east and west coasts, Las Vegas, The Comedy Store, and many more. After writing for several television programs on both the west and east coasts, Tom formed GPI Communications.

As a presentation coach, Tom has worked with architects, engineers, and designers. He has coached politicians, corporate executives, sales teams, teachers, and leadership teams in a variety of fields. He has worked with health care providers at Mercy Health System, Wagner Integrated Therapies, Mercy Hospital of Philadelphia, Keystone Mercy Health Plan, Robert Wood Johnson Hospital, and Thomas Jefferson Hospital.

As a marketing specialist, he has produced and directed over 400 TV spots and won a CLIO, among other awards. In broadcast TV, he has written and produced commercials for such clients as KFC, Disney, CBS, Universal Studios, and Keebler. He has worked with the top Fortune 500 companies helping them to improve their communications and presentations.

Tom has combined his unique experience as a performer and his knowledge of marketing to help his clients develop presentations that are memorable, motivational, and entertaining.

Index

OTHER TITLES IN THE BUSINESS CAREER DEVELOPMENT COLLECTION

Vilma Barr, Editor

- *Financing New Ventures* by Geoffrey Gregson
- *Strategic Bootstrapping* by Matthew W. Rutherford
- *Introduction to Business* by Patrice Flynn
- *Be Different!* by Stan Silverman

Announcing the Business Expert Press Digital Library

Concise e-books business students need for classroom and research

This book can also be purchased in an e-book collection by your library as

- a one-time purchase,
- that is owned forever,
- allows for simultaneous readers,
- has no restrictions on printing, and
- can be downloaded as PDFs from within the library community.

Our digital library collections are a great solution to beat the rising cost of textbooks. E-books can be loaded into their course management systems or onto students' e-book readers.
The **Business Expert Press** digital libraries are very affordable, with no obligation to buy in future years. For more information, please visit **www.businessexpertpress.com/librarians**. To set up a trial in the United States, please email **sales@businessexpertpress.com**.

CPSIA information can be obtained
at www.ICGtesting.com
Printed in the USA
BVHW040750020420
576404BV00013B/40

9 781951 527242